If America Were a Village

A Book about the People of the United States

Written by David J. Smith

Illustrated by Shelagh Armstrong

CitizenKid

A collection of books that inform children about the
world and inspire them to be better global citizens

Kids Can Press

This book is dedicated to some of the great teachers who taught me, or whose friendship and support helped model great teaching for me: Kathleen Raoul, Mary Eliot, Stan Sheldon, Ned Ryerson, Fritz Allis, Josh Miner, Frank DiClemente, Troy Horton, Arthur Robinson and Jane Goodall. And, always and forever, to Suzanne. — DS

To Paul and Caden for being so loving and patient while I worked. — SA

A note on the words "America" and "American"

"America" has several meanings. It may refer to a single country, the United States of America, or to the continent that includes not only the United States but also Canada, Mexico and all the countries of Central and South America. This land mass is often considered two continents — North America and South America — but many people in the world think of it as a single continent. The term "American" may refer to a citizen of any country on the continent, or of just the United States. For the purpose of this book, "America" refers only to the United States, and "American" refers to a person who lives in the United States.

Text © 2009 David J. Smith
Illustrations © 2009 Shelagh Armstrong

Kids Can Press acknowledges the financial support of the Government of Ontario, through the Ontario Media Development Corporation's Ontario Book Initiative; the Ontario Arts Council; the Canada Council for the Arts; and the Government of Canada, through the BPIDP, for our publishing activity.

Published in Canada by
Kids Can Press Ltd.
29 Birch Avenue
Toronto, ON M4V 1E2

Published in the U.S. by
Kids Can Press Ltd.
2250 Military Road
Tonawanda, NY 14150

www.kidscanpress.com

The artwork in this book was rendered in acrylic.
The text is set in Bodoni.

Edited by Valerie Wyatt
Designed by Marie Bartholomew
Printed and bound in China

This book is smyth sewn casebound.

CM 09 0 9 8 7 6 5 4 3 2 1

Library and Archives Canada Cataloguing in Publication

Smith, David J. (David Julian), 1944 –
    If America were a village : a book about the people of the United States / written by David J. Smith; illustrated by Shelagh Armstrong.

Includes bibliographical references.
ISBN 978-1-55453-344-2 (bound)

1. United States—Population—Juvenile literature.
2. Human geography—United States—Juvenile literature. I. Armstrong, Shelagh, 1961– II. Title.

HB3505.S56 2009   j304.60973   C2008-908125-0

Kids Can Press is a ʕOʀUs™ Entertainment company

Contents

Welcome to America

Bursts of color light up the sky. It is July 4, the day Americans celebrate Independence Day and the founding of their country. But who are the people who live in this vast and varied nation? Where did they come from? What are they like today? How do they compare with people in other countries of the world?

There are more than 306 million people in the United States today. This huge number is hard to imagine and even harder to analyze. And America never stays still— it is always changing and growing. There is 1 birth about every 8 seconds and 1 death every 12 seconds. A new immigrant arrives every 27 seconds. In total, 1 new person is added to the U.S. population every 12 seconds, which means that 1, or maybe even 2, were added while you were reading this paragraph.

To find out more about America and Americans, we are going to reduce the whole population of America to a village of 100 people, the imaginary village you see here. Each person in this village of 100 will represent more than 3 million Americans in the real world.

Let's enter the village and meet the people.

Who are we?

Look closely at the faces of the villagers and you will see a rainbow of colors. Americans come from all races and from all parts of the world. Some are newcomers, but others have been here for many generations.

In our village of 100:

• About 13 are foreign-born. Six of these have become U.S. citizens, while 7 are not yet citizens. Of the 13, 7 were born in Latin America, 2 were born in Europe, 3 in Asia. The remaining person (remember that 1 person represents 3 million Americans) comes from Africa, Canada and Oceania (an area that includes Australia, New Zealand and the islands of the south, west and central Pacific).

• 75 are white, 12 are black, 1 is Native American and 4 are Asian (including 1 from China and 1 from the Philippines). The remaining 8 consider themselves members of some other race or a mixture of races.

What languages do we speak?

• 82 people in our village speak English as their first language.

• 10 speak Spanish.

• 1 speaks Chinese, 1 French and 1 German.

Many other languages are important in the United States but are not widely enough spoken to represent 1 whole person in the village. From most widely spoken to least, these include Tagalog, Vietnamese, Italian, Korean, Russian, Polish, Arabic, Portuguese, Japanese, French Creole, African languages, Greek, Hindi, Persian, Urdu, Gujarati, Armenian, Hebrew, Khmer, Yiddish, Navajo, Hmong, Scandinavian languages, Laotian, Thai and Hungarian and many more.

Where do we come from?

America is a country of immigrants. Almost every person in the United States can trace ancestors back to other parts of the world.

If the America of today were a village of 100: 15 would be of German ancestry, 11 would be of Irish ancestry, 9 African, 9 English, 7 Mexican, 6 Italian, 3 Polish, 3 French, 3 Native American, 2 Scottish, 2 Dutch, 2 Norwegian, 1 Scotch-Irish and 1 Swedish. The rest have other backgrounds.

That is quite a change from when the first U.S. census was taken in 1790. If America had been a village of 100 in 1790, 53 would have come from England, 19 from Africa (most of them slaves), 11 from Scotland and Ireland and 7 from Germany. The rest had various backgrounds, including French, Swedish and Native.

Early on, most immigrants came from Europe, but that began to change after 1900:

- In 1900, 96 percent came from Europe, 1 percent from Latin America and 3 percent from other places.

- In 1950, 53 percent came from Europe, 40 percent from Latin America, 6 percent from Asia and 1 percent from other places.

- In 2000, 15 percent came from Europe, 49 percent came from Latin America, 31 percent from Asia and 5 percent from other places.

9

Where do we live?

Today, 80 of the 100 people live in cities and suburbs, while 20 live on farms and in the country. But it hasn't always been this way. A huge change has taken place in just 100 years.

During the 1900s, many Americans moved from the country to the city.

• In 1900, 40 people lived in towns and cities, and 60 lived in the country.

• In 1920, 51 lived in towns and cities, and 49 lived in the country.

• In 1940, 56 lived in towns and cities, and 44 lived in the country.

• In 1960, 70 lived in towns and cities, and 30 lived in the country.

• Today, 80 live in towns and cities, and 20 live in the country.

Americans move around a lot. In 2007, 17 of the 100 people moved. Of these 17, 11 moved within the same state, 5 moved to a different state and 1 moved to the United States from another country.

People are not evenly spread across the whole country. Americans like to live together, near other people. Of the 100 people:

• 50, half the population, live in just 9 states — 12 in California, 8 in Texas, 6 each in New York and Florida, 4 each in Illinois, Pennsylvania and Ohio, and 3 each in Michigan and Georgia.

• The remaining 50 people live in the other 41 states. The 5 least populated states account for a total of only 1 person. Yes, the populations of Wyoming, Vermont, North Dakota, Alaska and South Dakota all together add up to just over 3 million people, or 1 person in the U.S. village.

What are our families like?

When people think of an American family, they often imagine a mother, a father and 2 children. But in reality, American families come in all shapes and sizes.

In our imaginary village of 100:

- 20 families have 2 parents, while 7 are single-parent families. About half of these 27 families have children under the age of 18, for a total of 29 children.

- 10 households are made up of 1 person who lives alone.

- The remaining 14 people live in households of 2 or more unrelated people sharing living quarters.

About 1 percent of all families in America are made up of 2 people of the same sex, either 2 men or 2 women. Some of these same-sex couples also have children. But in the village as a whole, there are almost twice as many households without children as with.

How do American families compare with those of other nations? There are big differences. When young people in various countries were asked, "What's your ideal family? How many children do you want?" here's how they answered: In the United States, young people, on average, wanted 2 children; in India and Morocco, 5; in Yemen, Sudan and Kenya, 6; and in Mauritania, 9.

What religions do we practice?

There are many religions in America, but not all people are religious. If you asked the people in our village what religion they practice, here's what they would say:

- 82 consider themselves Christians. Of these, 54 are Protestants, 24 are Roman Catholics, 2 are Mormons and 2 practice other Christian religions.

- 2 are Buddhists.

- 1 is Jewish.

- 1 is Muslim.

- 4 practice a wide variety of other world religions (such as Baha'i, Sikhism and Taoism).

- 10 consider themselves non-religious.

About 40 people in the village attend a religious service every week.

Those numbers are quite different from the rest of the world. If the whole world were a village of 100 people, there would be:

- 32 Christians
- 20 Muslims
- 13 Hindus
- 11 who practice folk religions
- 6 Buddhists
- 2 who practice other global religions
- 1 Jewish person
- 15 who are non-religious

America has many more Christians than the world as a whole because of its history. Most of the early immigrants were from Christian countries, and they brought their religion with them.

What do we do?

Most days, the village is a busy place. The children are in school, and many of the adults are hard at work.

More than one-quarter of the inhabitants of our village — 27 in all — attend school. Three are in preschool or kindergarten, 12 are in elementary school, 6 are in high school and 6 are in college or other training.

Forty-seven people are employed. Of these:

- 18 are in professions:
    - 4 in management
    - 3 in education, training and library professions
    - 2 in health care
    - 2 in finance
    - 1 in computer technology
    - 1 in architecture and engineering
    - 5 in science, law, social service and the arts

- 12 are in sales, selling goods or services in stores or offices

- 7 are in service occupations:
    - 2 in food preparation
    - 2 in cleaning and maintenance of building and grounds
    - 1 in health care support
    - 1 in firefighting and law enforcement
    - 1 in personal care and services (barbers, beauticians, etc.)

- 5 work in construction and repair, building or fixing buildings and products

- 5 work in manufacturing, farming and the transportation of goods

There are 5 people in the village who want to work but can't find jobs, and that number may be rising. The remaining 21 people don't work: 15 are retired, while 6 are not looking for work or are unable to work. Of the 6, 1 person is in prison or jail. (One other, who may be working, is on parole from prison.)

18

How old are we?

As you wander through the village, you will see people of all ages, from babies to the elderly. The U.S. population is slightly older than that of the rest of the world, and it is getting older every year.

Here is how the ages of people in our village of 100 compare to those of the world as a whole.

Age	U.S.	World
0 to 9	13	19
10 to 19	14	18
20 to 29	14	17
30 to 39	14	15
40 to 49	15	12
50 to 59	13	9
60 to 69	8	6
70 to 79	5	3
80+	4	1

So if the *world* were a village of 100, 37 people would be younger than 20, while in the U.S. village, that number would only be 27.

Why is the United States aging faster than the world as a whole? One explanation is that many women in America postpone having children because they are in the workforce. As a result, fewer babies are being born and therefore there are fewer young people in total.

How wealthy are we?

Every country has wealthy people and poor people.

In our U.S. village of 100:

• 5 people have more than half of all the wealth.

• The 1 wealthiest person (and remember, 1 person represents 3 million people in the real America) has more than 30 percent of all the wealth.

• The 60 poorest people share only about 4 percent of the wealth.

Many people in our village live below the poverty line — they make less money than is required to meet their food, shelter and clothing needs. And the number of people living in poverty is increasing. In 2000, there were 11 people living below the poverty line; in 2004, there were 12. In 2008, 14 people in the U.S. village lived below the poverty line.

Still, America is wealthier than many other countries. One measure of a country's wealth is the gross domestic product (GDP) per person. This is the number you get if you take the value of all the goods and services sold in a country in one year and divide it by the population. In the United States, the GDP per person is almost $46 000, while worldwide it's just $10 200. America is the 9th richest country in the world. As a comparison, the GDP per person in the world's poorest country, Burundi, is just $127.

Some regions of America are much richer than others. The state of Delaware has the highest average income per person: about $70 000. The lowest is in Mississippi at less than half that: around $28 000. There are also differences between men's and women's incomes in America. For every dollar a man earns, a woman earns only 77 cents.

What do we own?

Americans own lots of stuff. In our village of 100 people, there are:

- 81 cars, more than in any other country. If the whole *world* were a village of 100 people, there would be only 13 cars, and 3 of those would be in the United States. In some countries, including Ethiopia, Mali, Madagascar, Nigeria, Afghanistan and Malawi, there would be just 1 car or less per 100 people.

- 73 cell phones, about the same number as in Barbados, Bermuda and Japan. If the *world* were a village of 100 people, there would be about 50 cell phones, and 4 of those would be in the United States. But Americans are not the top users of cell phones; 18 countries now have more cell phones than people, with the highest number, 158 per 100 people, in Luxembourg.

- 74 televisions. If the *world* were a village of 100 people, there would be 25 televisions, and 4 of those would be in the United States. But again, though America has a lot of TVs, it doesn't have the most. Bermuda comes first, with 101, and Monaco is second, with 77. There are many countries, including Eritrea, Chad, Tanzania and Bangladesh, that have less than 1 television in their village of 100.

What else do Americans own? In the U.S. village, there are 200 radios, 76 computers, 39 bicycles and 40 portable media players, such as MP3 players.

24

What do we use?

No matter where in the world you live, you need energy and water. America uses a lot of both.

Americans use more energy than any other country in the world. If all the energy sources — coal, petroleum, natural gas, nuclear, renewable, electricity — were added up, Americans would use 21 percent of the world's total. Here's how America compares to some other countries in energy use:

United States 〇〇〇〇〇〇〇〇〇〇〇〇〇〇〇〇〇〇〇〇〇 21.4%

China 〇〇〇〇〇〇〇〇〇〇〇〇〇〇〇 15.6%

Russia 〇〇〇〇〇〇 6.5%

Japan 〇〇〇〇 4.8%

India 〇〇〇 3.9%

Canada 〇〇〇 3%

Germany 〇〇〇 3%

In America, energy is used in industry, for transportation and for other needs at home and at work. Wood was the main source of energy until the end of the 1800s, when it was replaced by coal and then by petroleum. Today, gas for cars and trucks accounts for two-thirds of all the petroleum used in the United States.

Americans are also the world's top users of water. Water is used in homes, for irrigating crops and for industrial processes. You'd need an Olympic-sized swimming pool to hold the water each American uses, on average, each year — about 456 000 gallons (1 726 140 L). Americans use more water per person than any other country in the world. In Greece, the rate per person is half that amount, and in the United Kingdom it's only about one-eighth.

Here are some other things Americans use in just one day:

• 4 million plastic cups and 39 million paper cups

• 576 million plastic beverage bottles, of which 60 million are recycled

• more than 1 billion plastic bags

• more than 4 billion sheets of paper

How healthy are we?

A child born today in the U.S. village can expect to live to nearly 78 years of age. A hundred years ago, the life expectancy was only 48 years. This is a huge improvement, but the United States is far from being the world's number 1 country for life expectancy — in fact, it is number 40. At the top of the list is Andorra: a baby born there can expect to live 83.5 years. At the other extreme are 5 countries with life expectancies of less than 40 years: Lesotho (39.9 years), Zimbabwe (39.5), Zambia (38.4), Angola (37.6) and Swaziland (32.2). The lowest 36 countries are all in Africa.

Health is closely linked to good nutrition. Americans are, by and large, pretty lucky when it comes to food. But 13 people in the village are considered food insecure, which means they have trouble finding resources to put food on the table. Eighty-seven people do have access to adequate food. Sixty-five people are overweight.

The people in the U.S. village are healthier than in many other places, but not as healthy as they could be. Even though America spends more money on heath care than any other country, the United States ranks number 37 for quality of health care, after Dominica and Costa Rica and just ahead of Slovenia and Cuba.

America past and future

Before Europeans arrived, as many as 10 million Native people may have been living in North America (Canada, Mexico and the United States). Over time, that number dropped, as Native people died of disease or were killed in wars. Meanwhile, more and more people came to America from other parts of the world.

If the U.S. were a village of 100 today, here's how big the village would have been over time:

Before 1492	3
1700	less than 1
1800	1
1850	8
1900	25
1950	50
2000	93
Today	100

What will America be like in the future? By 2050, the population is predicted to be about 419 million, about one-third larger than today. If that population were shrunk to a village of 100, there would be 72 whites (including 24 Hispanics), 15 blacks, 8 Asians and 5 who identify themselves as members of other races.

As it has in the past, America will continue to grow and change.

Before 1492

1800

1850

1900

Today

29

Helping our children understand America

America is a land of incredible diversity and complexity, and making sense of it is no easy task. Although Americans are often united by shared beliefs, fears and hopes for the future, they are also more than 306 million individuals who go to some lengths to maintain their individuality. The people who live here are not all alike, nor are they easily categorized or defined.

If America Were a Village is an attempt to take a statistical snapshot of America — past, present and future — to make it more comprehensible to children. By reducing the entire population to a village of 100, we can see the various groups and the similarities and differences among them. We can also compare America with other countries to see what similarities and differences this reveals.

The village of 100 is a powerful and accessible tool to use with children. Instead of huge numbers, 100 is a manageable number that can be easily comprehended. To make the numbers even more real for children, use 100 felt or paper cutouts of people (or use 100 stones or pennies) and work your way through each page. The differences and divisions become clearer, and sometimes more surprising, when they are set out in this way.

How else can we help our children understand America and Americans more clearly? How can we examine what distinguishes America from other countries and Americans from other people?

Here are a few ways to support our children in unraveling this complex, multi-faceted and interesting place.

• Read with children about other parts of the United States and the world. There are a vast number of books available at all age levels. A good selection is maintained at http://www.mapping.com/resources.html, and your local children's librarian can help you find other titles. Through books, children will see that some people and places are like them, while others are very different — even within the United States.

• Keep maps and globes around the house or classroom. Use them with your children — and let your children use them by themselves. Keep track of family travels on a map. Locate family members. Every time a new place is mentioned in conversations, on the news or in a book, look it up, locate it. Ask: "What do you think it's like there?" Help your kids find an answer to that question.

• Look and explore. As you walk around your community, think about humans and their surroundings. Ask questions such as, "Which of these things were here before there were any people?" "Which things were put here by people?" or "Why are there three gas stations, a bank and a drugstore on this corner and nothing in the rest of the block?" It's easier for children to grasp the complexities of American geography and culture if they can see that there is a reason for things being the way they are.

• As you listen to music, watch films and read books with your children, talk about what you see, hear and learn. Our understanding of American society, geography and people are all improved by paying attention to modern and popular culture.

• Help children understand that America is physically huge and varied. Ask questions such as, "If it's dusk here in Miami, what time of day is it in California?" In a grocery store, look at where produce comes from and when and how. Check the weather in various parts of the country and notice the differences. For example, in the northern U.S., weather usually comes from the west to the east. Check the weather 1000 miles west of where you live and see if it moves toward you.

• See how America trades with its neighbors. The question "Where did our eggs and milk originate?" will have a very different answer from "Where did our shoes originate?" Where do the products — and the people — in our neighborhood and our country come from?

• Travel around the U.S., or talk about traveling, in different ways, by different methods—walking, by car, bus, bicycle, train or airplane. How does each method differ from the others—what can you see, or not see, with each one? How long would the same trip take? Plan a driving route across the country based on a theme, such as capital cities, national parks, lakes, mountains and so on.

• Celebrate your own cultural heritage and talk about it, but also notice and talk about the other celebrations going on around you during the year. As you're getting ready to celebrate Christmas, one neighbor celebrates Hanukkah and another fasts for Ramadan. You celebrate Passover, while a friend celebrates Easter or has fresh lamb for Eid. Ask your neighbors about their cultures and share your customs with them. Look for similar customs in different cultures. Make connections for your children.

• America is a land of symbolism, often defining itself by its symbols. Have children examine some American symbols. Look closely at the Great Seal. What do the parts of it mean? Let children design their own seals — for themselves or for their family, school or country. Read about or visit the Statue of Liberty. What does it symbolize? What do the words on the pedestal mean? Design another statue. What would a Statue of Wisdom look like or a Statue of Tolerance or a Statue of Imagination? One important symbol of America is Uncle Sam. Look at images of him. Talk with children about his clothes and his attitude. What does he symbolize? Why is there an Uncle Sam but no Aunt Sandra? Talk about the flag. What do the parts of it symbolize? What about the colors?

• Another American symbol is the national anthem. America celebrates itself as "the land of the free and the home of the brave." How do other countries portray themselves? "O Canada" mentions "true patriot love" and asks God to "keep our land glorious and free." The British ask God to "save our gracious queen." Australia's national anthem, "Advance Australia Fair," begins "… let us rejoice, for we are young and free." South Africa's "Nkosi sikelel' iAfrika" says, "God bless Africa … God bless us." In its English translation, the national anthem of Kenya says, "Let all with one accord, In common bond united, Build this our nation together." In Brazil, they sing "in thy lovely, smiling and clear skies the image of the Southern Cross shines resplendently."

• Enter the words "compare the U.S. to other countries" on any search engine and you'll get thousands of links to Web sites comparing health data, income taxes, crime and punishment, energy use, banking and hundreds of other topics, even the cost of airline tickets and the amount of work professionals do. For example, the OECD issued a report recently showing that U.S. teachers spend 25 percent more time in the classroom than teachers from the 29 other OECD member countries. Looking at these comparisons can teach us a lot about our own country and our global neighbors.

Which brings me to what I think is the real point of this book. While unique in many ways, America shares many attributes and hopes with other countries, and the people of the U.S. are very much like people anywhere. Moreover, we are part of many communities — our local community, our national community, our world community. But our sense of community sometimes seems to be fraying. People see the issues that divide us rather than the ties that bind us.

As adults, we need to encourage children's sense of their own local community and their appreciation of the other communities to which they belong. Maybe this will help them come to a wider view of the world—a view that sees the common ground we share and allows us to work and live together. It is my hope that this book will enrich and improve that sense of community—not just who we are, where we live and what we do and believe, but also where others live and what they do and what they believe—and that kids will then be inspired to find ways to make their country and their world a better place.

David J. Smith

A note on sources

Many Web sites and books were used to compile the statistics for this book. I generally began my research using Web sites of various organizations. As a rule, I used data from a Web site only if I could verify the data in print. The organizations whose Web sites I used, and their top-level Web addresses, are listed below, followed by full citations for my print sources. Not all sources agreed. If necessary, averages or extrapolations have been made from related information.

The most important of the Web sites I used follow. I recommend them to teachers and researchers for their amazing archives of data.

United States Government Web sites:

Census Bureau:
http://www.census.gov

Bureau of Labor Statistics:
http://www.bls.gov

Justice Department:
http://www.justice.gov

Department of Energy:
http://www.eia.doe.gov

Environmental Protection Agency:
http://www.epa.gov

Citizenship and Immigration Service: http://www.uscis.gov

Bureau of Transportation Statistics:
http://www.bts.gov

Department of Agriculture:
http://www.usda.gov

United Nations Web sites:

Department of Economic and Social Affairs:
http://www.un.org/esa/desa

Development Program:
http://www.undp.org

Food and Agriculture Organization:
http://www.fao.org

European Union Web sites:

Environment Agency:
http://www.eea.europa.eu

Statistics Office: http://epp.euro-stat.ec.europa.eu

Other organizations' Web sites:

The Population Reference Bureau:
http://www.prb.org

The World Bank:
http://www.worldbank.org

The World Resources Institute:
http://www.wri.org

Worldwatch Institute:
http://www.worldwatch.org

The Modern Language Association:
http://www.mla.org

The primary print sources were as follows:

U.S. Census Bureau, *Statistical Abstract of the United States*, Government Printing Office, Washington, DC, 2008 (and earlier editions).

U.S. Central Intelligence Agency, *CIA World Factbook*, Skyhorse Publishing, New York, 2008, and earlier editions published by Potomac Books, Dulles, VA (2007 and earlier).

The World Bank, *World Development Report*, Oxford University Press and The World Bank, Washington, DC, 2007 (and earlier editions).

The World Bank, *World Development Indicators*, World Bank Publications, Washington, DC, 2007 (and earlier editions).

United Nations Department of Economic and Social Affairs, *World Population Prospects*, United Nations, New York, various years 1998–2006.

World Health Organization, *World Health Report*, United Nations World Health Organization, New York, 1998–2006.

Centers for Disease Control, "National Vital Statistics Reports," U.S. Department of Health and Human Services, Superintendent of Documents SuDoc HE 20.6217, Washington, DC, 2007 (and earlier editions).

National Marriage Project, "The State of Our Unions," Rutgers University, New Brunswick, NJ, 2002–2007.

Frey, Abresch and Yeasting, *America by the Numbers*, The New Press, New York, 2001.

The Worldwatch Institute, *State of the World*, W.W. Norton, New York, 2007 (and earlier editions).